ORIGAMI
Birds

Duy Nguyen

Sterling Publishing Co., Inc.
New York

Design by Judy Morgan
Edited by Claire Bazinet

Library of Congress Cataloging-in-Publication Data

Nguyen, Duy, 1960 –
  Origami birds / Duy Nguyen.
      p. cm.
  Includes index.
  ISBN-13: 978-1-4027-1932-5
  ISBN-10: 1-4027-1932-9
  1. Origami. 2. Birds in art. I. Title.

TT870.N4864 2006
736'.982– dc22

                                            200503766910

9 8 7 6 5 4 3 2 1

Published by Sterling Publishing Co., Inc.
387 Park Avenue South, New York, NY 10016
© 2006 by Duy Nguyen
Distributed in Canada by Sterling Publishing
c/o Canadian Manda Group, 165 Dufferin Street, Toronto, Ontario, Canada M6K 3H6
Distributed in the United Kingdom by GMC Distribution Services
Castle Place, l66 High Street, Lewes, East Sussex, England BN7 1XU
Distributed in Australia by Capricorn Link (Australia) Pty. Ltd.
P.O. Box 704, Windsor, NSW 2756, Australia

Printed in China
Sterling ISBN-13: 978-1-4027-1932-5
       ISBN-10: 1-4027-1932-9

For information about custom editions, special sales, premium
and corporate purchases, please contact Sterling Special Sales
Department at 800-805-5489 or specialsales@sterlingpub.com.

Contents

Preface

Years ago, when I began to fold origami, I would look at the instructions for even the simplest folds again and again. But I also looked ahead, at the diagram showing the next step of whatever project I was folding, to see how it *should* look. As it turned out, looking ahead at the next step, the result of a fold, is a very good way for a beginner to learn origami.

You will easily pick up this learning technique and many others as you follow the step-by-step directions given here for creating a whole array of birds—an aviaryful, if you wish.

So sit down, select some paper, begin to fold…and enjoy the wonderful art that is origami.

Duy Nguyen

Basic Instructions

Paper: Paper used in traditional origami is thin, keeps a crease well, and folds flat. Packets of specially designed sheets, about 6 and 8 inches (15 and 21 cm) square, are available in various colors. A number of the bird-shaped projects given here call for rectangular paper, but this shouldn't be a problem. You can use plain white, solid-color, or even wrapping paper with a design only on one side and cut the paper to size. Be aware, though, that some papers stretch slightly in length or width, which can cause folding problems, while others tear easily.

Beginners or those concerned about working with smaller tight folds can use larger paper sizes. While regular paper may be a bit heavy to allow making many tight folds used in creating traditional origami figures, it is fine for working larger projects.

Technique: Fold with care. Position the paper, especially at corners, precisely and line edges up before creasing. Once you are sure of the fold, use a fingernail to make a clean, flat crease.

For more complex folds, create "construc-tion lines." Fold and unfold, using simple mountain and valley folds, to pre-crease. This creates guidelines, and the finished fold is more likely to match the one shown in the book. At this stage, folds that look different, because the angles are slightly different, can throw you off. Don't get discouraged with your first efforts. In time, what your mind can create, your fingers can fashion.

Creativity: Fold several of the same bird. Do you really want them all to look exactly alike? Once you are more confident in your folding ability, try adjusting certain folds to shape the form more to your liking, bringing each bird to life in your hands.

Do add color and detail, too. I have freely used markers, glued on bits and folds of paper, even spray painted figures for variety. To make several bird forms shown in this book more colorful and realistic, I have first folded the forms, used markers to color-mark them, then opened and scanned the forms into a computer. Drawing over the scanned images and adding color produced printed patterns—ready for final folding.

Symbols & Lines

Fold lines	valley	- - - - - -	
	mountain	-·-·-·-	

Fold then unfold

Cut line   +++++++++++

Pleat fold
(repeated folding)

Turn over or rotate

Crease line

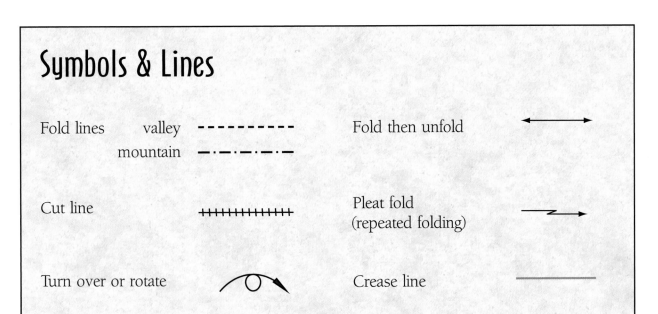

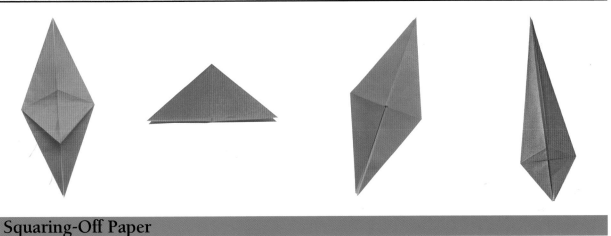

Squaring-Off Paper

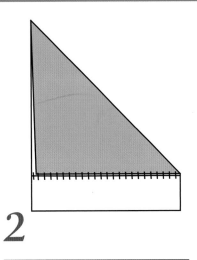

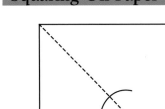

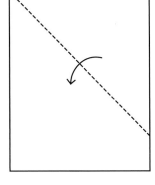

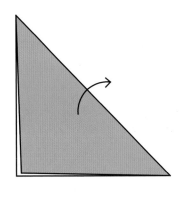

1
Take a rectangular sheet
of paper and valley fold it
diagonally to opposite edge.

2
Cut off excess on long side
as shown.

3
Unfold, and sheet is square.

Basic Folds

Kite Fold

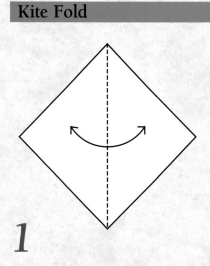

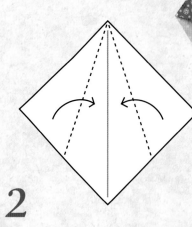

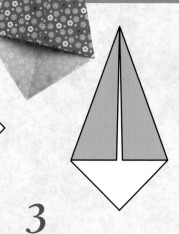

1
Fold and unfold a square diagonally, making a center crease.

2
Fold both sides in to the center crease.

3
This is a kite form.

Valley Fold   ------------------

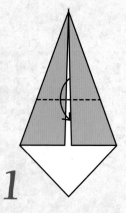

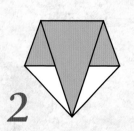

1
Here, using the kite, fold form toward you (forwards), making a "valley."

2
This fold forward is a valley fold.

Mountain Fold   —·—·—·—·—

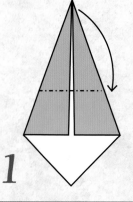

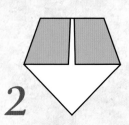

1
Here, using the kite, fold form away from you (backwards), making a "mountain."

2
This fold backward is a mountain fold.

Basic Folds

6

Inside Reverse Fold

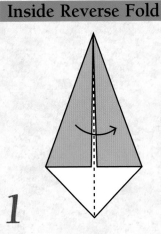

1

Starting here with a kite, valley fold kite closed.

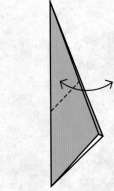

2

Valley fold as marked to crease, then unfold.

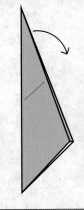

3

Pull tip in direction of arrow.

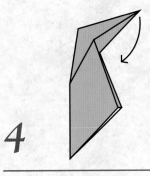

4

Appearance before completion.

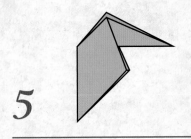

5

You've made an inside reverse fold.

Outside Reverse Fold

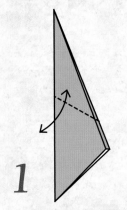

1

Using closed kite, valley fold, unfold.

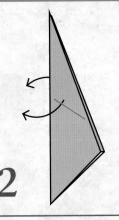

2

Fold inside out, as shown by arrows.

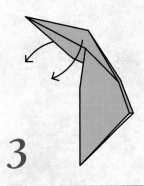

3

Appearance before completion.

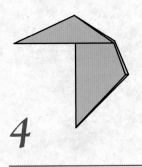

4

You've made an outside reverse fold.

Pleat Fold

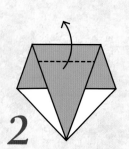

1

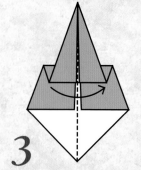

2

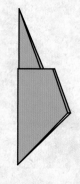

3

4

Here, using the kite, valley fold.

Valley fold back again.

This is a pleat. Valley fold in half.

You've made a pleat fold.

Pleat Fold Reverse

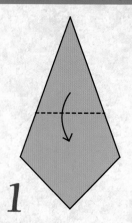

1

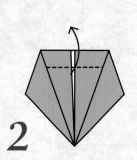

2

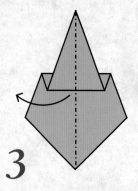

3

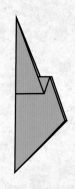

4

Here, using the kite form backwards, valley fold.

Valley fold back again for pleat.

Mountain fold form in half.

This is a pleat fold reverse.

Squash Fold I

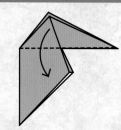

1

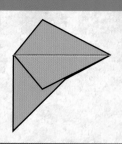

2

Using inside reverse, valley fold one side.

This is a squash fold I.

Squash Fold II

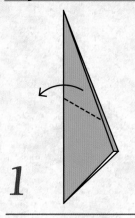

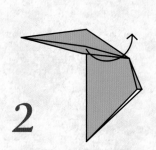

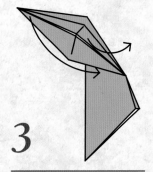

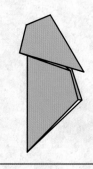

1 Using closed kite form, valley fold.

2 Open in direction of the arrow.

3 Appearance before completion.

4 You've made a squash fold II.

Inside Crimp Fold

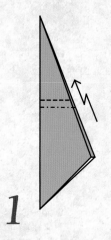

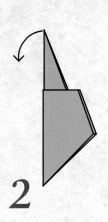

1 Here, using closed kite form, pleat fold.

2 Pull tip in direction of the arrow.

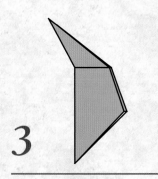

3 This is an inside crimp fold.

Outside Crimp Fold

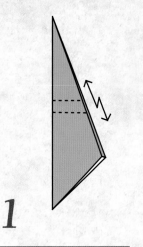

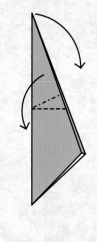

1 Here, using closed kite form, pleat fold and unfold.

2 Fold mountain and valley as shown, both sides.

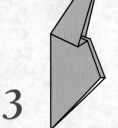

3 This is an outside crimp fold.

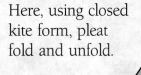

Basic Folds

Base Folds

Base folds are basic forms that do not in themselves produce origami, but serve as a basis, or jumping-off point, for a number of creative origami figures—some quite complex. As when beginning other crafts, learning to fold these base folds is not the most exciting part of origami. They are, however, easy to do, and will help you with your technique. They also quickly become rote, so much so that you can do many using different-colored papers while you are watching television or your mind is elsewhere. With completed base folds handy, if you want to quickly work up a form or are suddenly inspired with an idea for an original, unique figure, you can select an appropriate base fold and swiftly bring a new creation to life.

Base Fold I

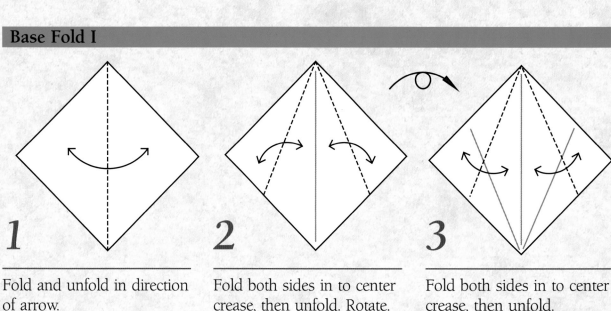

1 Fold and unfold in direction of arrow.

2 Fold both sides in to center crease, then unfold. Rotate.

3 Fold both sides in to center crease, then unfold.

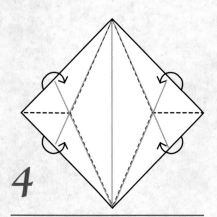

4 Pinch corners of square together and fold inward.

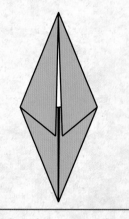

5 Completed Base Fold I.

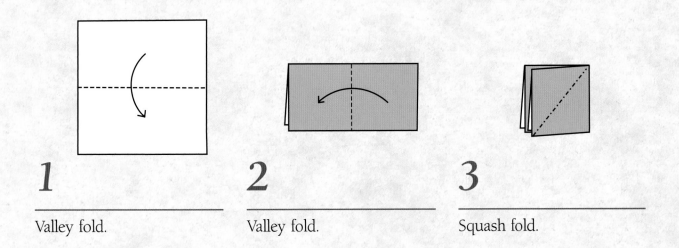

1
Valley fold.

2
Valley fold.

3
Squash fold.

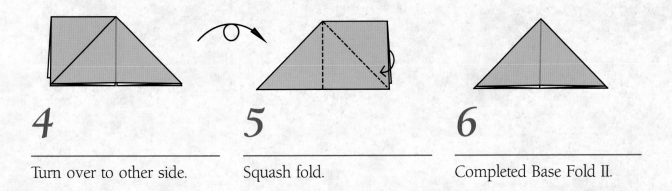

4
Turn over to other side.

5
Squash fold.

6
Completed Base Fold II.

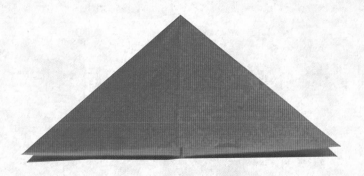

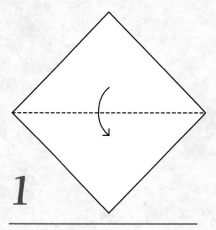

1

Valley fold.

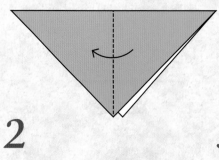

2

Valley fold.

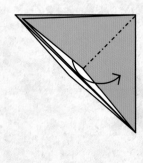

3

Squash fold.

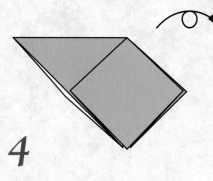

4

Turn over.

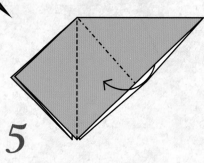

5

Squash fold.

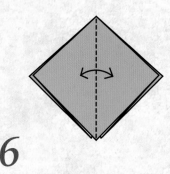

6

Valley fold, unfold.

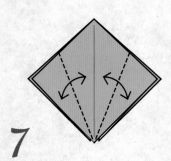

7

Valley folds, unfold.

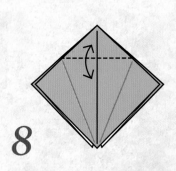

8

Valley fold, unfold.

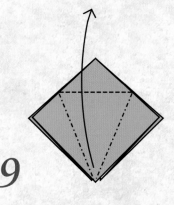

9

Pull in direction of arrow, folding inward at sides.

Base Folds

10

Appearance before completion of fold.

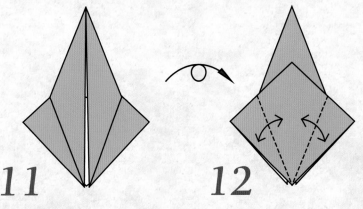

11

Fold completed. Turn over.

12

Valley folds, unfold.

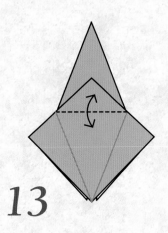

13

Valley fold, unfold.

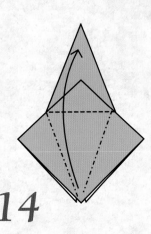

14

Repeat, again pulling in direction of arrow.

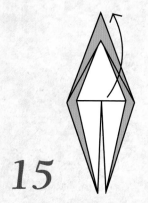

15

Appearance before completion.

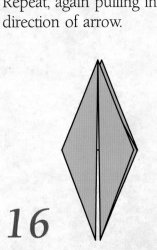

16

Completed Base Fold III.

1

Valley fold rectangle in half as shown. (Note: Base Fold IV paper size can be variable, but 4" by 11" is used for birds throughout book.)

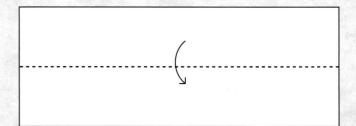

2

Valley fold in direction of arrow.

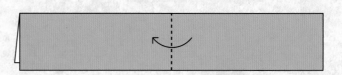

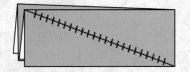

3

Make cut as shown

4

Unfold.

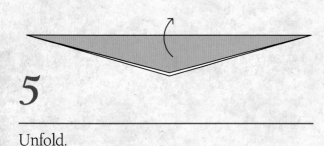

5

Unfold.

6

Valley fold in half.

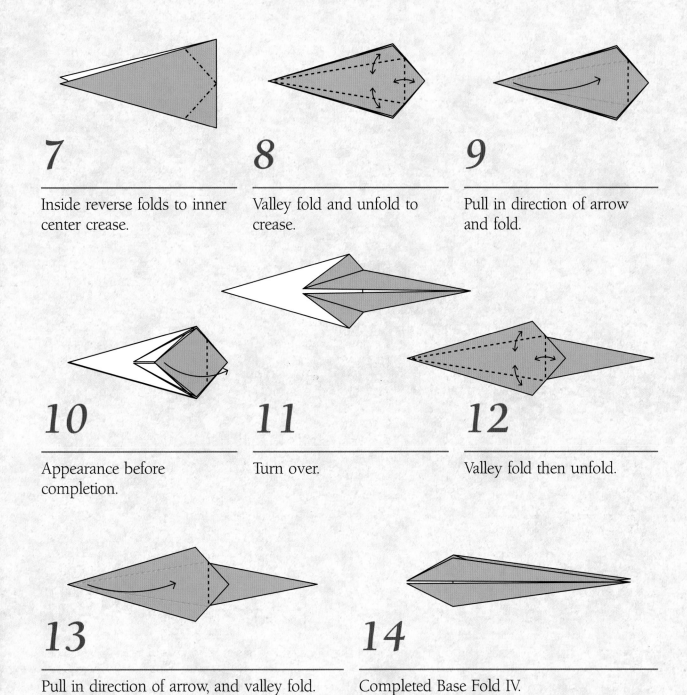

7

Inside reverse folds to inner center crease.

8

Valley fold and unfold to crease.

9

Pull in direction of arrow and fold.

10

Appearance before completion.

11

Turn over.

12

Valley fold then unfold.

13

Pull in direction of arrow, and valley fold.

14

Completed Base Fold IV.

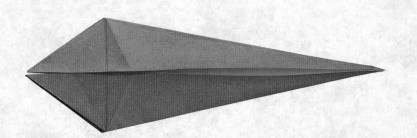

Penguin

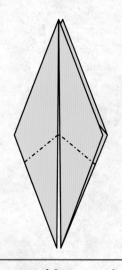
1

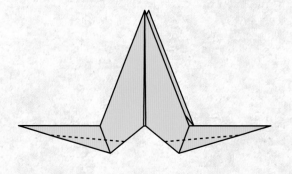

Start with Base Fold III. Inside reverse folds.

2

Valley folds.

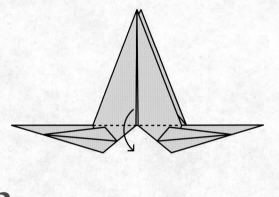

3

Valley fold.

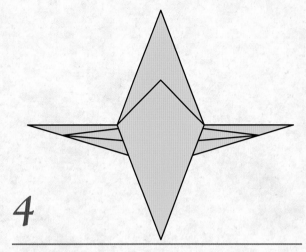

4

Valley folds.

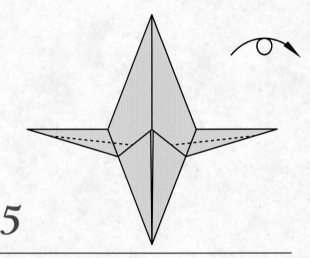

5

Turn over to other side.

6

Valley fold in half.

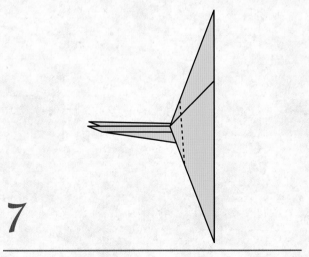

7

Valley fold both sides.

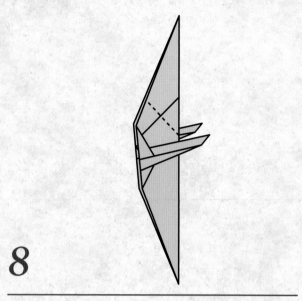

8

Inside reverse fold.

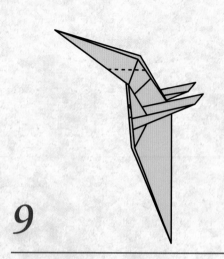

9

Outside reverse fold.

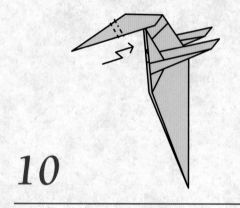

10

Pleat fold.

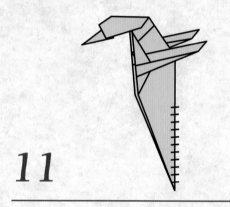

11

Cut as shown.

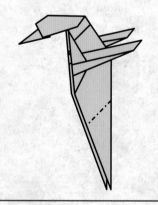

12

Mountain fold both sides.

13

Add coloring if you wish.

14

Completed Penguin.

Turkey

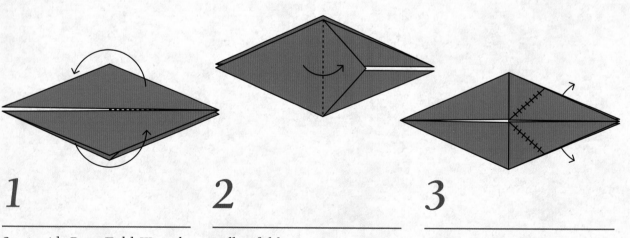

1

Start with Base Fold III and
valley fold both sides.

2

Valley fold.

3

Make cuts as shown, then
valley folds.

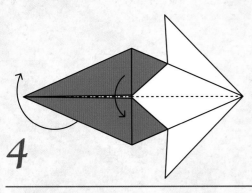

4

Valley fold both front and back.

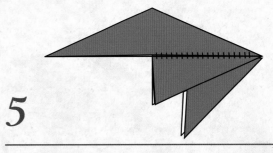

5

Make cuts front and back.

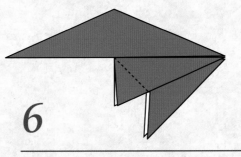

6

Valley fold cut parts both sides.

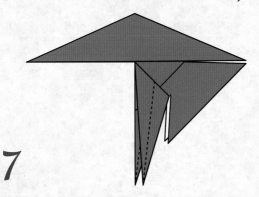

7

Valley fold both front and back.

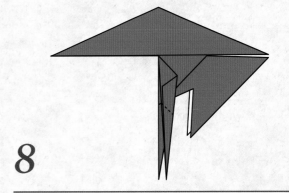

8

Outside reverse folds front and back.

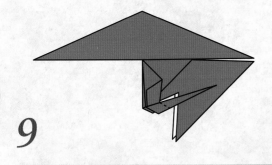

9

Outside reverse folds front and back.

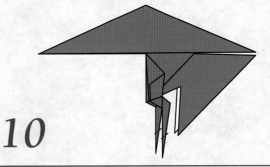

10

Inside reverse folds front and back.

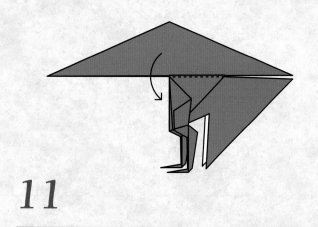

11

Valley fold both sides in direction of arrow.

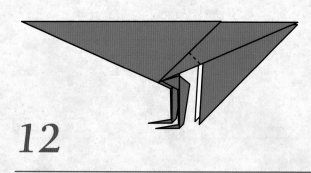

12

Valley folds front and back.

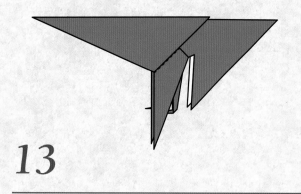

13

Valley folds front and back.

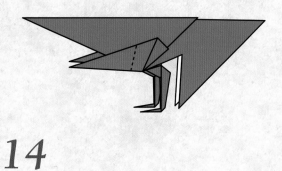

14

Valley folds front and back.

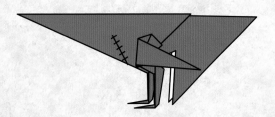

15

Cuts as shown, to both sides.

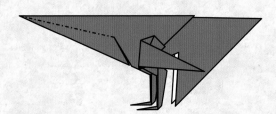

16

Mountain folds front and back.

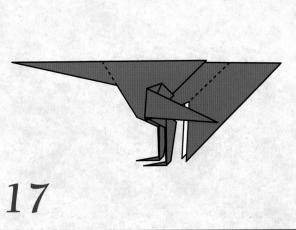

17

Outside reverse folds.

18

Outside reverse fold.

19

Cut edge, then valley fold.

20

Mountain fold.

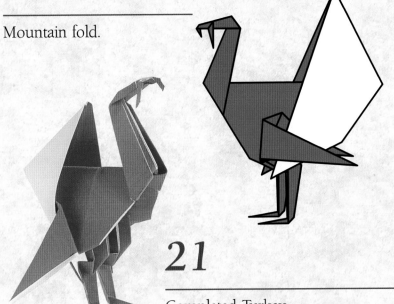

21

Completed Turkey.

Tricolored Heron

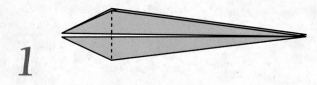

1

Start with Base Fold IV made from 4" by 11" paper. Valley fold both front and back.

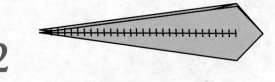

2

Cut front layer.

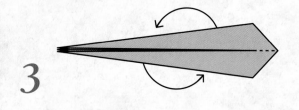

3

Valley fold to open flaps.

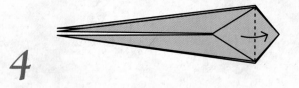

4

Valley fold both front and back.

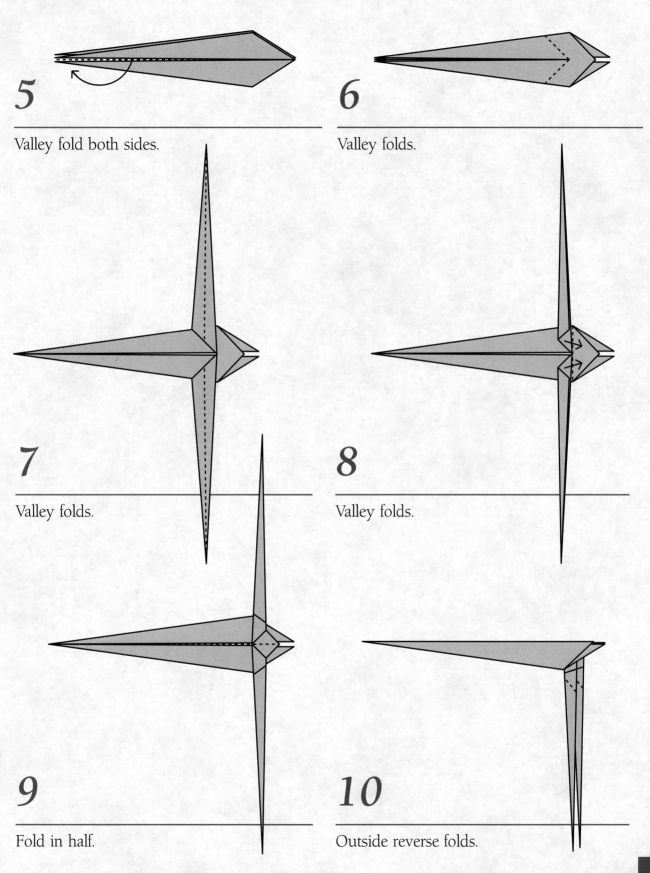

5

Valley fold both sides.

6

Valley folds.

7

Valley folds.

8

Valley folds.

9

Fold in half.

10

Outside reverse folds.

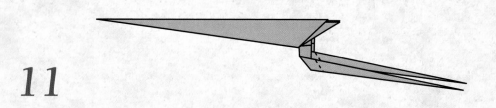

11

Outside reverse folds both front and back.

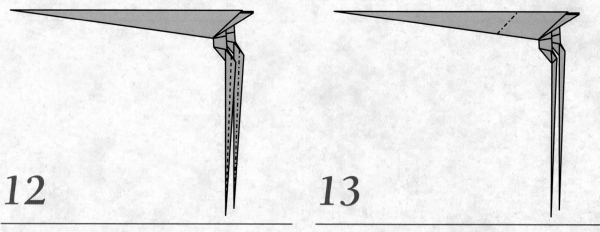

12

Valley fold both sides.

13

Inside reverse fold.

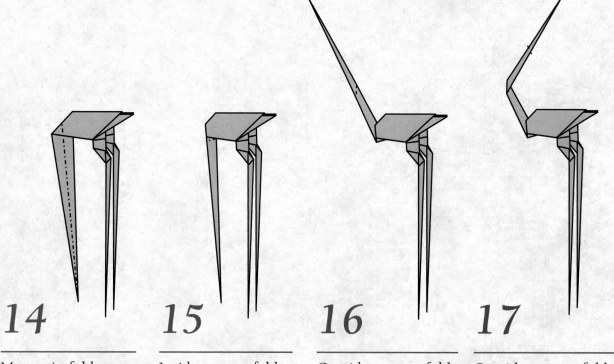

14

Mountain fold.

15

Inside reverse fold.

16

Outside reverse fold.

17

Outside reverse fold.

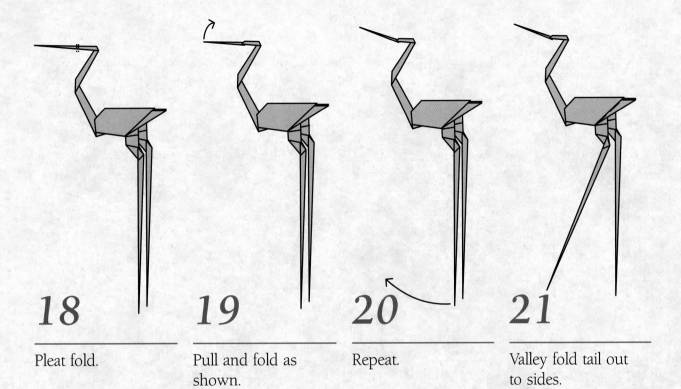

18
Pleat fold.

19
Pull and fold as
shown.

20
Repeat.

21
Valley fold tail out
to sides.

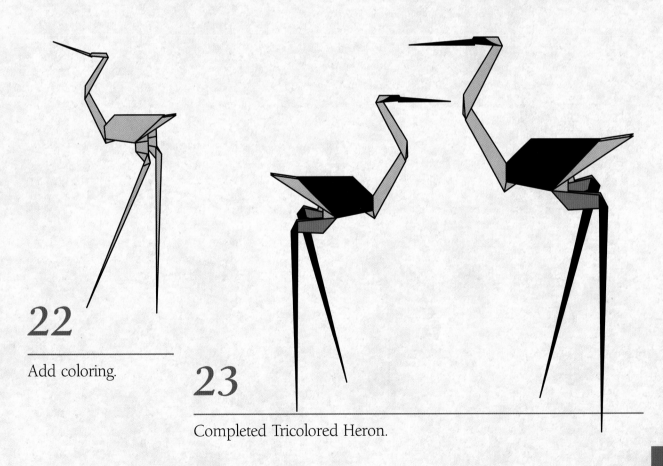

22
Add coloring.

23
Completed Tricolored Heron.

Stork

Part 1

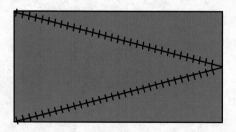

1

Start with 5.5" by 4" paper. Cut as shown.

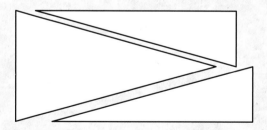

2

Separate the pieces, and select the center piece.

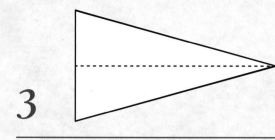

3

Valley fold and unfold.

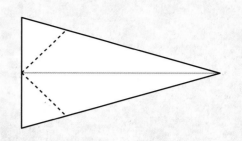

4

Valley fold.

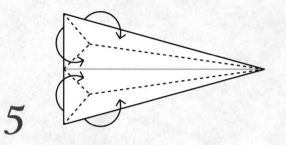

5

Pinch the corners together and valley fold the sides inward.

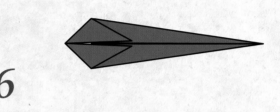

6

Unfold.

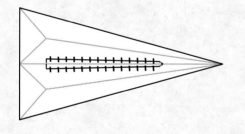

7

Make cuts as shown.

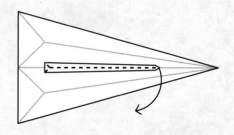

8

Pinch to valley fold center flap. Pull in direction of arrow.

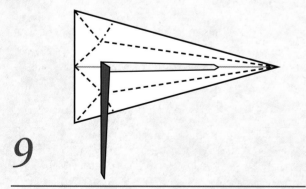

9

Repeat the step 5 folds.

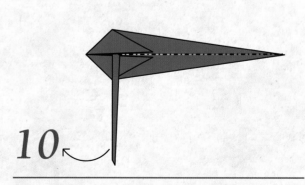

10

Mountain fold the lower portion in half upward, and pull the flap to the left.

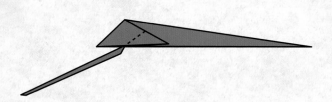

11

Valley fold both front and back.

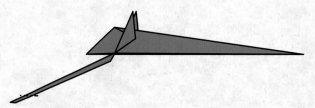

12

Inside reverse fold.

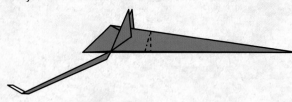

13

Crimp fold.

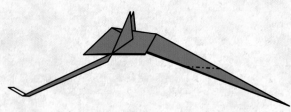

14

Inside reverse fold.

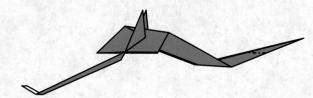

15

Inside reverse fold.

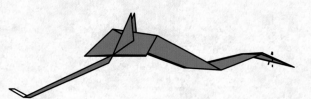

16

Crimp fold.

17

Completed part 1 of stork.

1

Select a triangular piece.
Valley fold and unfold.

2

Valley fold.

3

Repeat with second piece.
Completed wing sections.

1

Join all parts together and
apply glue to hold.

2

Valley fold wings outward.

3

Mountain fold wings.

4

Make cuts as shown to trim
and "feather" wings. Stretch
wings outward.

5

Add coloring and detail.

6

Completed Stork.

Stork

31

Hummingbird

Part 1

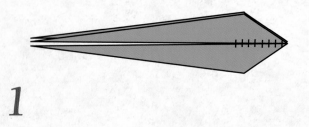

1

Start with step 5 of Tricolored Heron. Cut front and back as shown, but *do not cut* center layer.

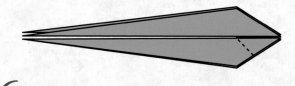

6

Valley fold both front and back.

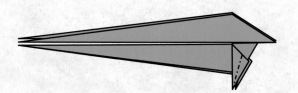 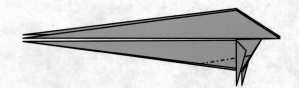

7

Inside reverse fold both sides.

8

Mountain fold both front and back.

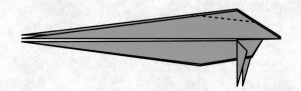 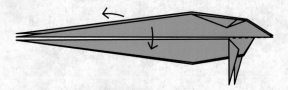

9

Valley fold both sides.

10

Valley fold both front and back.

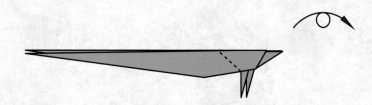

11

Valley fold both sides. Rotate.

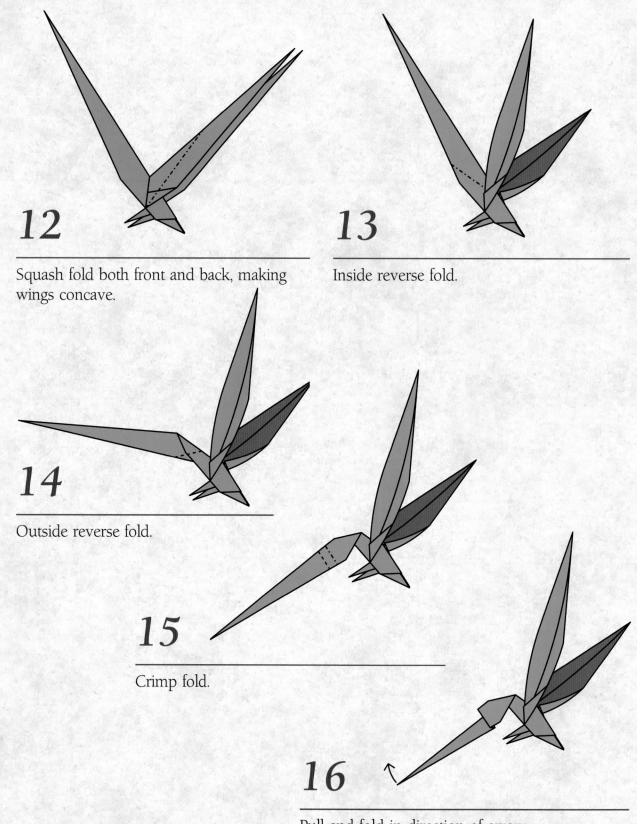

12

Squash fold both front and back, making wings concave.

13

Inside reverse fold.

14

Outside reverse fold.

15

Crimp fold.

16

Pull and fold in direction of arrow.

17

Mountain fold both front and back.

18

Mountain fold both sides. Add coloring...
and supply with flowers.

19

Completed Hummingbird.

Goose

Standing Goose

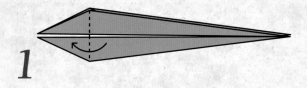

1

Start with Base Fold IV, using 4" by 11" paper. Valley fold both sides

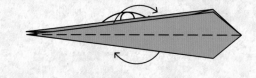

2

Valley fold to open flaps.

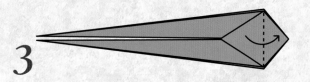

3

Valley fold both front and back. .

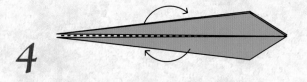

4

Valley fold back to step 2 position.

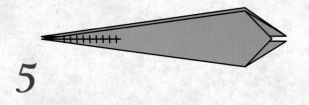

5

Make cut to front layer only.

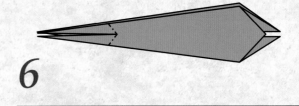

6

Mountain fold.

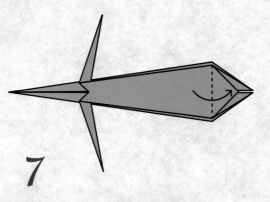

7

Valley fold.

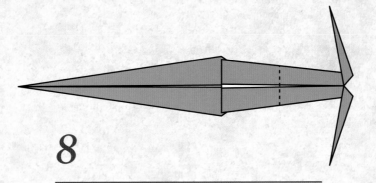

8

Valley fold.

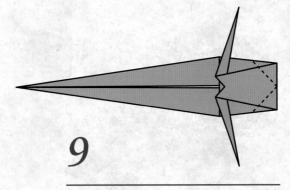

9

Valley folds.

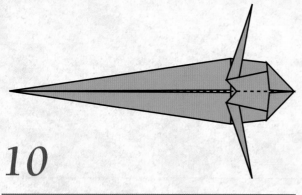

10

Valley fold.

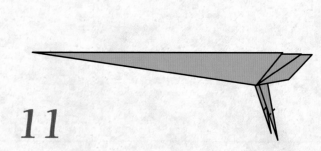

11

Outside reverse fold.

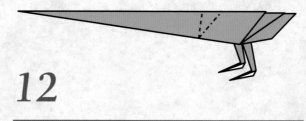

12

Crimp fold.

13

Mountain fold.

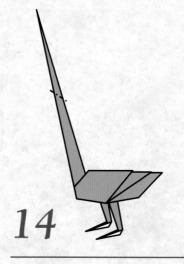

14

Inside reverse fold.

15

Outside reverse fold.

16

Pull layers from inside flaps and squash fold open.

17

Pleat fold.

18

Pull and crimp.

19

Cut as shown.

20

Mountain fold both sides.

21

Add coloring and pattern.

22

Completed Goose (standing).

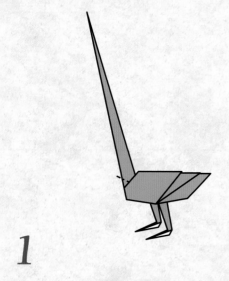

1

Work through to step 14 of Standing Goose (pages 36–38). Inside reverse fold.

15

Inside reverse fold.

16

Inside reverse fold.

17

Cut front layer only, on each side.

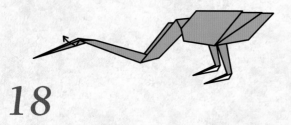

18

Valley fold cut part on both sides.

19

Pleat fold.

Goose

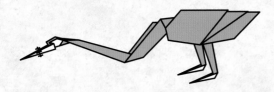

20

Cut as shown.

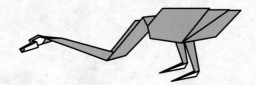

21

Mountain fold beak tip front and back.

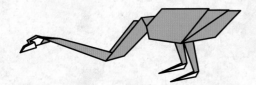

22

Add coloring.

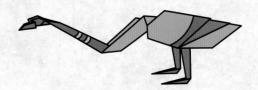

23

Completed Goose (feeding).

Mockingbird

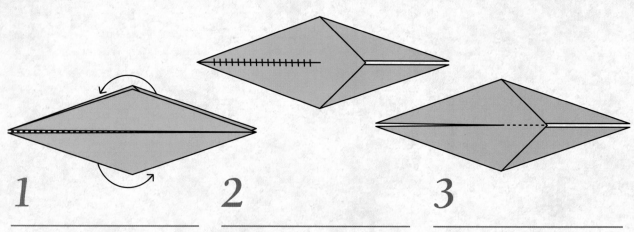

1

Start with Base Fold III. Valley fold both sides.

2

Cut as shown on both sides.

3

Valley folds to return to step 1 position.

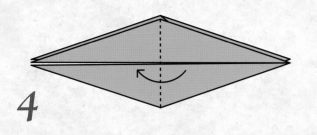

4

Valley fold top layer.

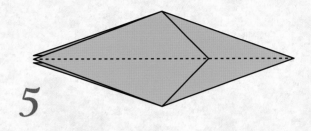

5

Valley fold in half.

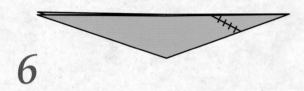

6

Cut top layers front and back.

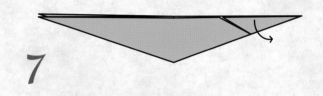

7

Valley open cut parts.

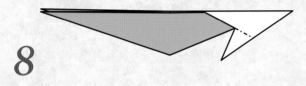

8

Mountain fold both front and back.

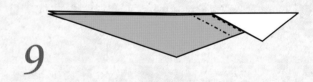

9

Crimp fold.

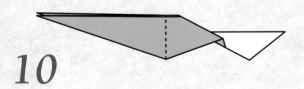

10

Valley fold both front and back.

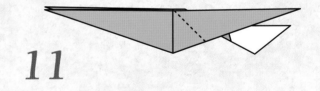

11

Valley fold both front and back.

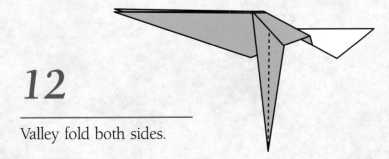

12

Valley fold both sides.

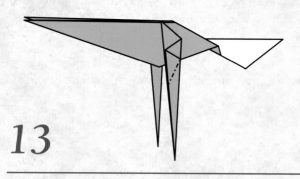

13

Inside reverse folds front and back.

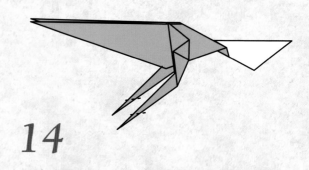

14

Outside reverse folds both sides.

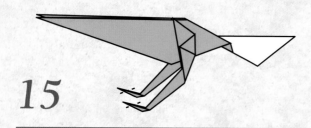

15

Outside reverse folds.

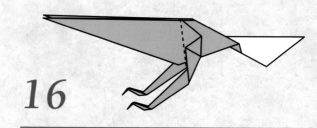

16

Valley folds both front and back.

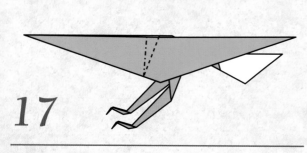

17

Crimp fold.

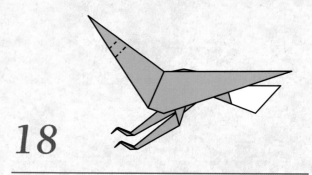

18

Crimp fold.

19

Pull into position and squash fold.

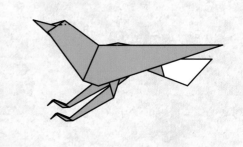

20

Inside reverse fold.

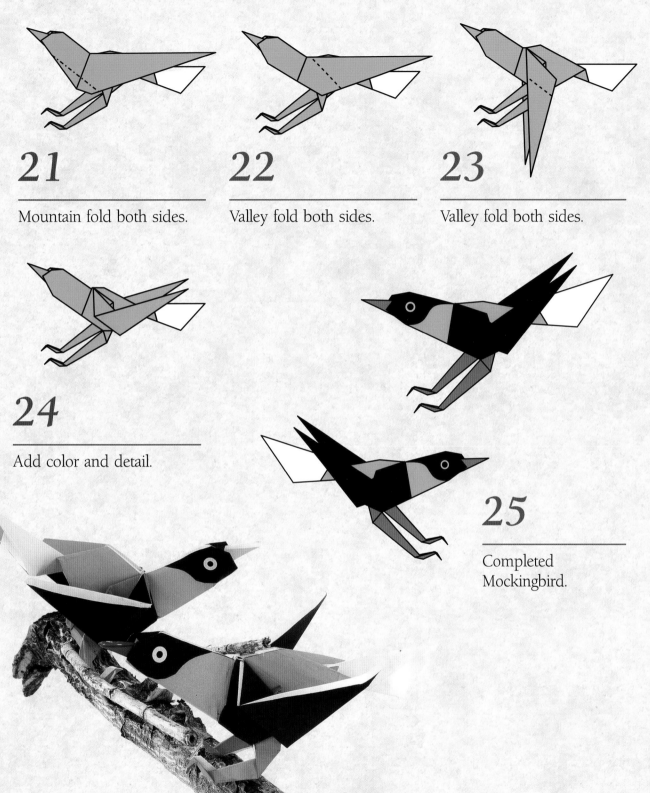

21

Mountain fold both sides.

22

Valley fold both sides.

23

Valley fold both sides.

24

Add color and detail.

25

Completed
Mockingbird.

Snake Bird

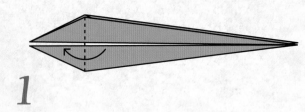

1

Start with Base Fold IV. Valley fold both sides as shown.

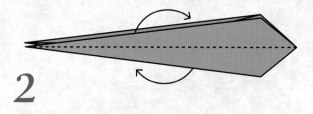

2

Valley fold front and back to open flaps.

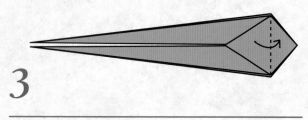

3

Valley folds, both front and back.

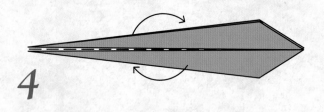

4

Valley folds front and back to close flaps.

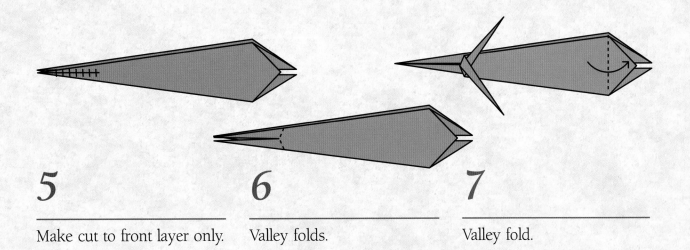

5

Make cut to front layer only.

6

Valley folds.

7

Valley fold.

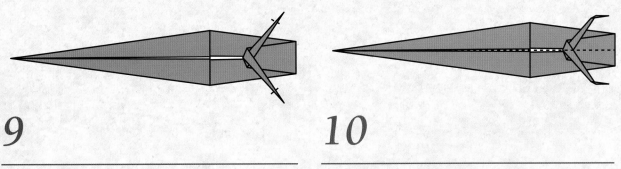

8

Valley fold.

9

Valley folds.

10

Valley fold in half.

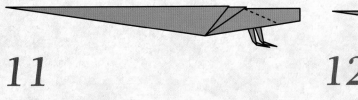
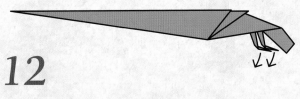

11

Inside reverse fold.

12

Pull and squash fold as shown.

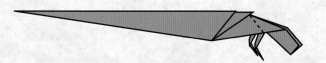

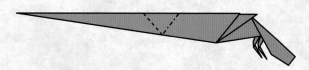

13

Valley fold both sides.

14

Crimp fold.

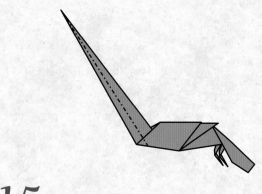

15

Mountain folds, both front and back.

16

Crimp fold.

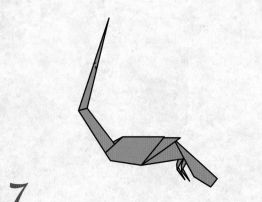

17

Inside reverse fold.

18

Outside reverse fold.

19

Pleat fold.

20

Pull and squash fold, then add
color or detail.

21

Completed Snake Bird.

Pelican

Part 1

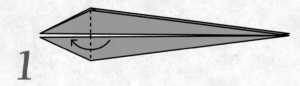

1

Start with Base Fold IV. Valley fold both front and back.

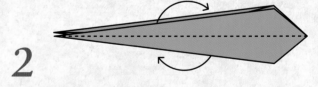

2

Valley fold both sides to open flaps.

3

Valley folds, both front and back.

4

Valley folds back to step 2 position.

5

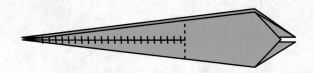

Cut front layer and valley fold cut parts.

6

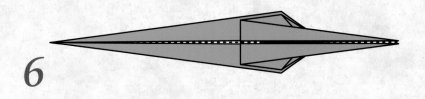

Mountain fold in half.

7

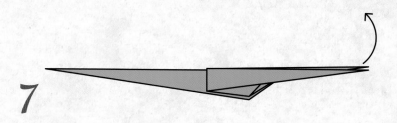

Pull both sides as shown and squash fold into position.

8

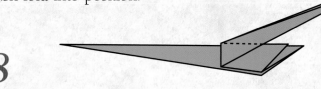

Valley fold both front and back.

9

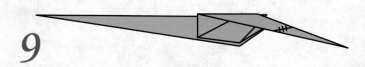

Make cuts both front and back.

10

Outside reverse fold.

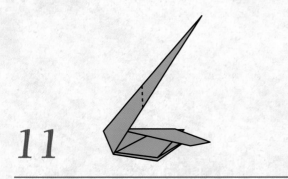

11

Outside reverse fold.

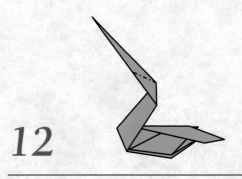

12

Inside reverse fold.

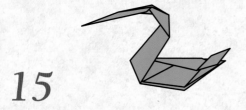

13

Outside reverse fold.

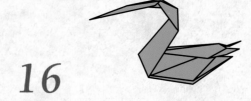

14

Valley fold both sides.

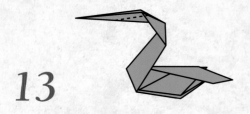

15

Unfold to balance both sides.

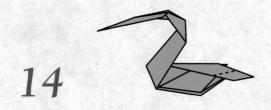

16

Completed part 1 of pelican.

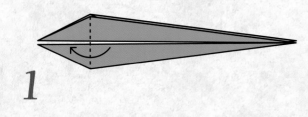

1

Start with Base Fold IV. Valley fold both sides.

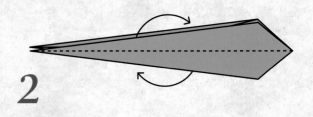

2

Valley fold both sides to open flaps.

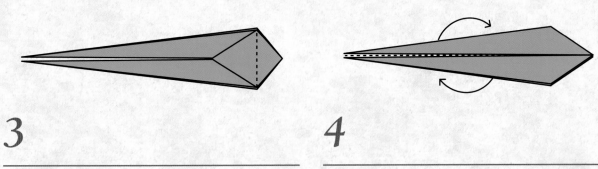

3

Valley folds, both front and back.

4

Valley folds back to step 2 position.

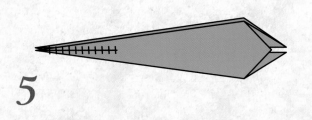

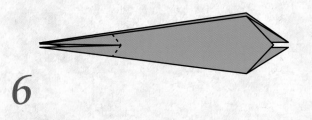

5

Make cut to front layer only.

6

Outside reverse folds.

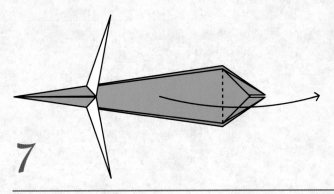

7

Valley fold in direction of arrow.

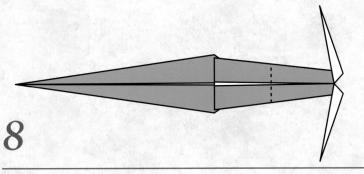

8

Valley fold.

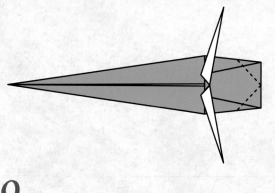

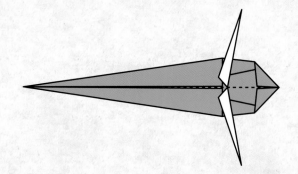

9

Valley folds.

10

Valley fold.

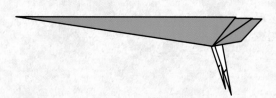

11

Outside reverse folds.

12

Outside reverse folds.

13

Outside reverse fold.

14

Inside reverse fold.

15

Cut outer layer on both sides.

16

Valley fold both cut parts.

17

Outside reverse fold.

18

Completed part 2 of pelican.

To Attach

1

Join both parts together as shown and apply glue to hold.

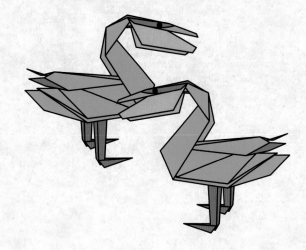

2

Cut both tips to shape beak.

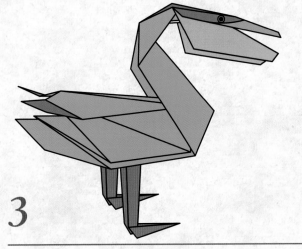

3

Completed Pelican.

Cardinal

Part 1

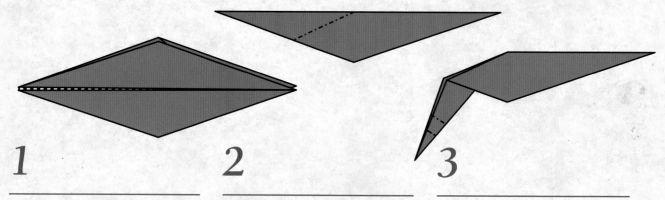

1

Start with Base Fold III.
Valley fold in half.

2

Inside reverse fold both flaps
together.

3

Crimp fold outer flap only.

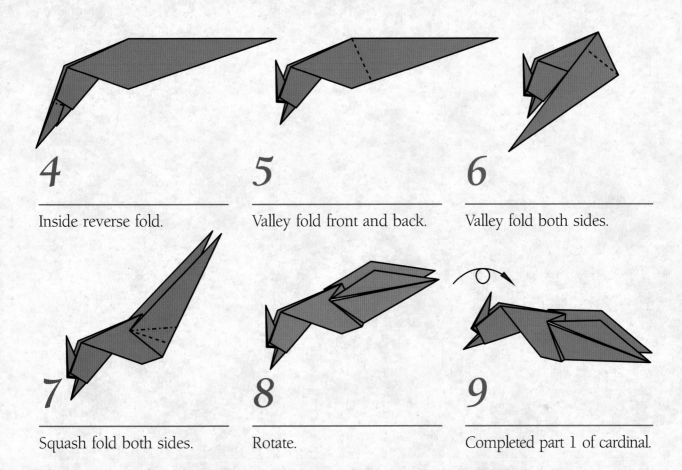

4

Inside reverse fold.

5

Valley fold front and back.

6

Valley fold both sides.

7

Squash fold both sides.

8

Rotate.

9

Completed part 1 of cardinal.

Part 2

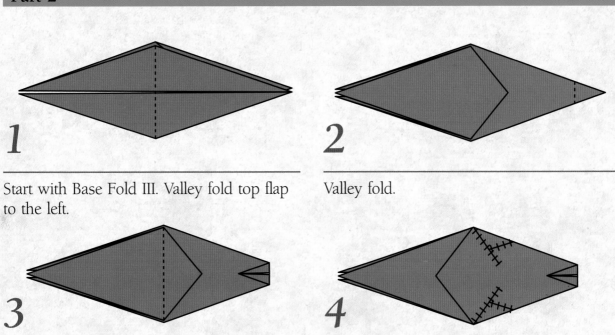

1

Start with Base Fold III. Valley fold top flap to the left.

2

Valley fold.

3

Valley fold.

4

Make cuts as shown.

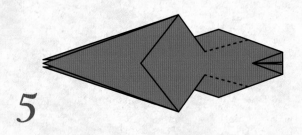

5

Valley fold cut parts.

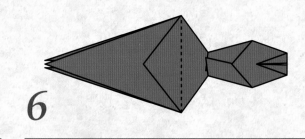

6

Valley fold.

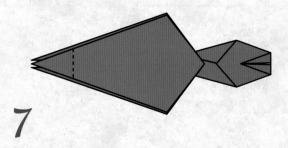

7

Valley fold.

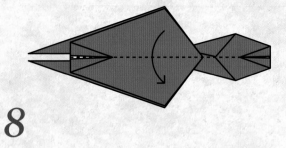

8

Valley fold in half.

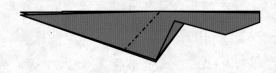

9

Inside reverse fold, both front and back.

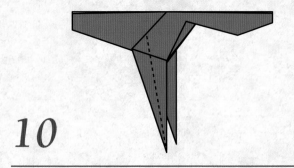

10

Valley fold both sides.

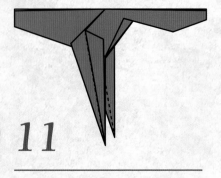

11

Mountain folds.

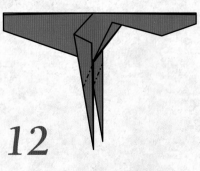

12

Inside reverse fold both sides.

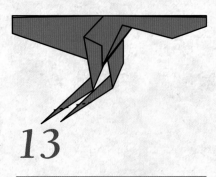

13

Outside reverse folds.

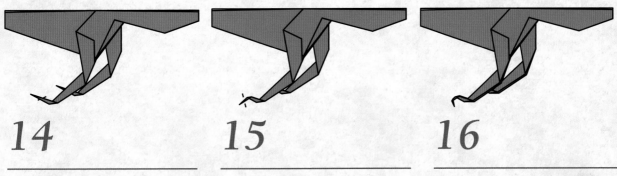

14

Inside reverse fold both sides.

15

Inside reverse fold both sides.

16

Completed part 2 of cardinal.

To Attach

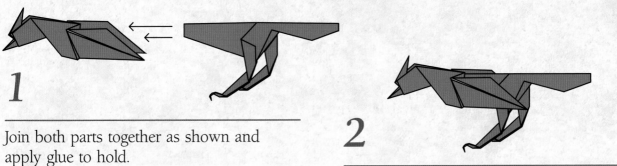

1

Join both parts together as shown and apply glue to hold.

2

Add colors and patterning to completion.

3

Completed Cardinal.

Parrot

Part 1

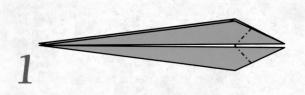

1

Start with Base Fold IV. Inside reverse folds.

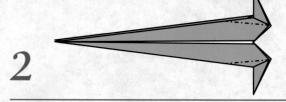

2

Mountain fold both sides.

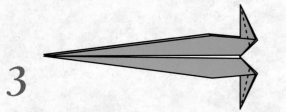

3

Valley fold both sides.

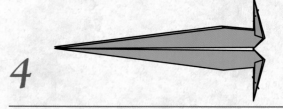

4

Inside reverse folds.

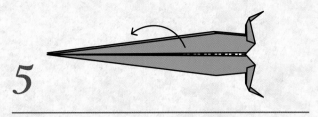

5

Mountain fold in half.

6

Outside reverse fold top layer.

7

Cut as shown.

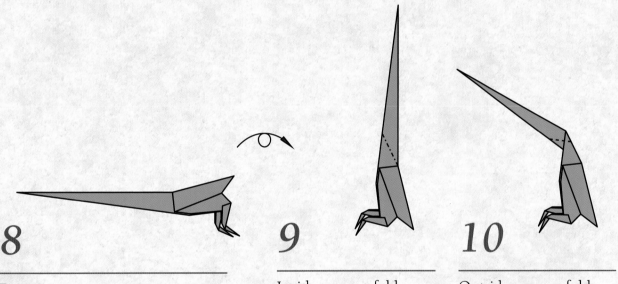

8

Rotate.

9

Inside reverse fold.

10

Outside reverse fold.

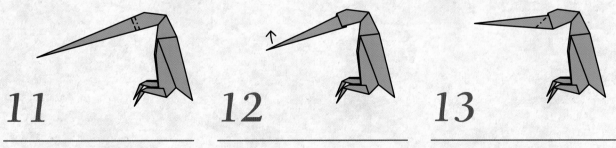

11

Pleat fold.

12

Pull and squash to crimp.

13

Inside reverse fold.

14

Cut through all layers.

15

Cut on fold to separate.

16

Completed part 1
of parrot.

Part 2

1

Start with Base Fold IV. Valley fold both
sides.

2

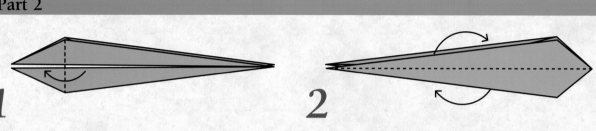

Valley fold front and back to open flaps.

3

Valley folds, front and back.

4

Valley fold back to step 2 position.

5

Valley fold.

6

Valley fold and squash.

7

Valley fold and squash.

8

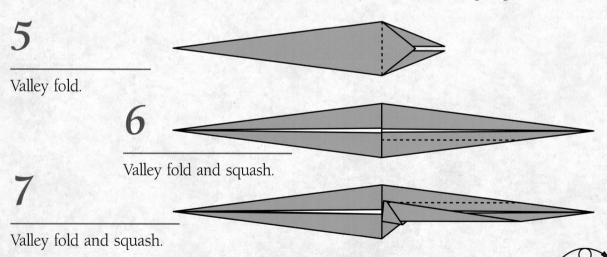

Valley fold and rotate.

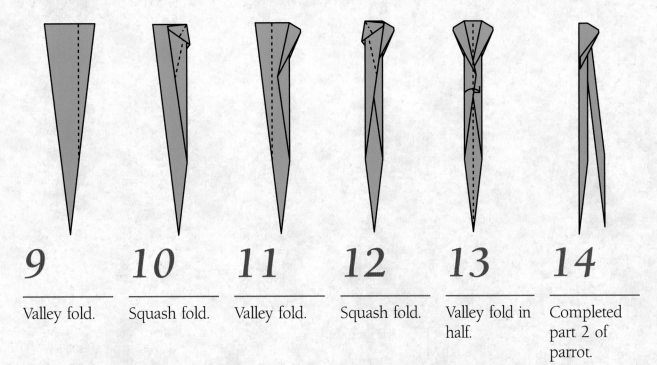

9
Valley fold.

10
Squash fold.

11
Valley fold.

12
Squash fold.

13
Valley fold in half.

14
Completed part 2 of parrot.

To Attach

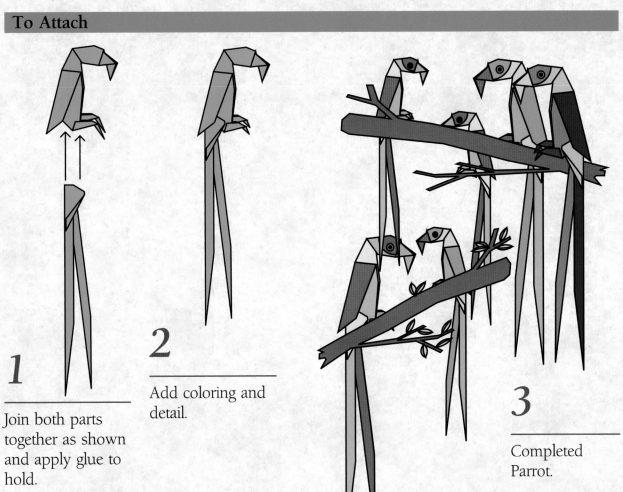

1
Join both parts together as shown and apply glue to hold.

2
Add coloring and detail.

3
Completed Parrot.

Falcon

Note: When making Base Fold IV for this project, save corner triangles of 4" by 11" paper for wing parts 3 and 4 (see page 70).

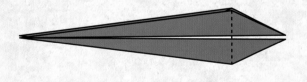

1

Start with Base Fold IV. Valley fold.

2

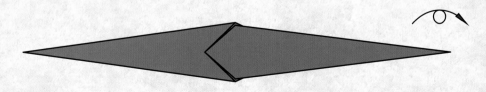

Turn over to other side.

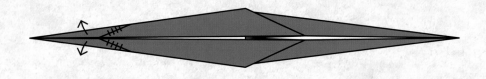

3

Cuts to top layers and valley fold cut parts.

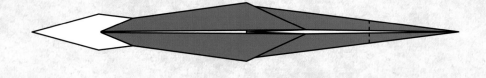

4

Valley fold and unfold to crease.

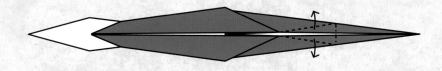

5

Open out at shown and squash fold at crease.

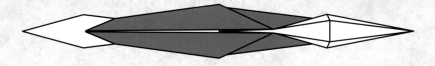

6

Appearance before completion.

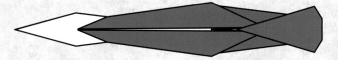

7

Bring lower layers to top.

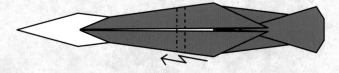

8

Pleat fold to crease.

9

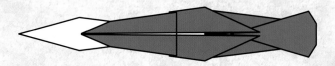

Unfold.

10

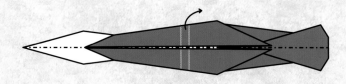

Mountain fold in half.

11

Crimp fold at creases.

12

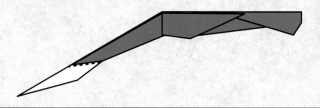

Outside reverse fold.

13

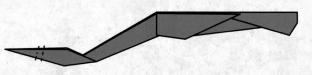

Crimp fold.

14

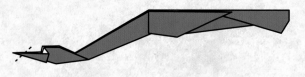

Outside reverse fold.

15

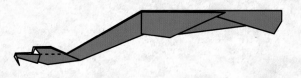

Valley fold both front and back.

16

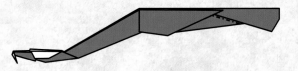

Inside reverse fold.

17

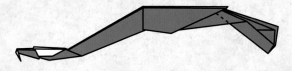

Valley fold both front and back.

18

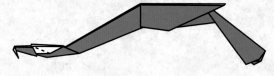

Valley fold both front and back.

19

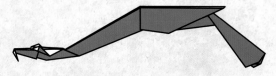

Completed part 1 of falcon.

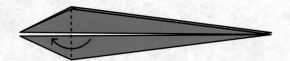

1

Start with Base Fold IV. Valley fold both sides.

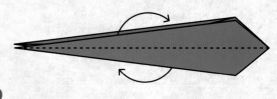

2

Valley fold to open flaps.

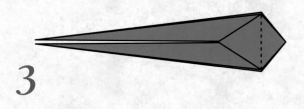

3

Valley folds, both sides.

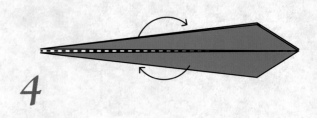

4

Valley fold to return to step 2 position.

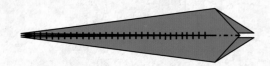

5

Cut front layer only as shown, then mountain fold form in half.

6

Mountain fold both sides as shown.

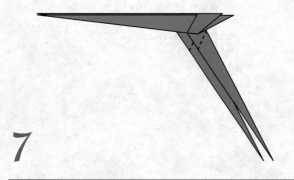

7

Valley fold both sides.

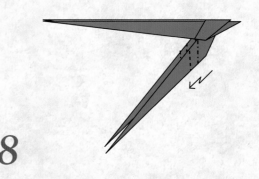

8

Pleat fold both front and back.

Falcon

9

Valley fold both front and back.

10
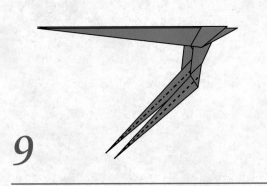

See blow-up for more detail.

11

Inside reverse folds.

12

Valley open folds.

13

Valley folds.

14

Valley folds.

15

Inside reverse folds.

16

Mountain folds. Back to full view.

17
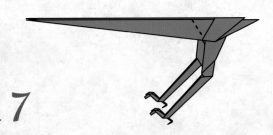

Valley fold both front and back.

18

Completed part 2 of falcon.

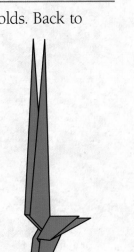

Falcon

1

From corners cut from Base
Fold IV, select upper triangle.

2

Cut one section as shown.

3

Completed part 3, left wing section.

4

Cut other section as shown.

5

Completed part 4, right wing section.

Right Wing

Left Wing

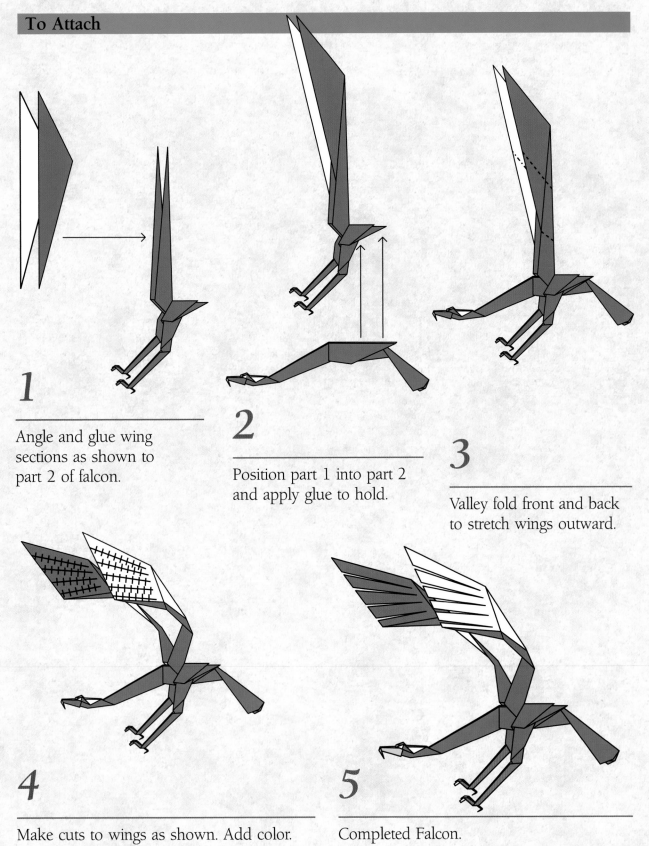

1

Angle and glue wing sections as shown to part 2 of falcon.

2

Position part 1 into part 2 and apply glue to hold.

3

Valley fold front and back to stretch wings outward.

4

Make cuts to wings as shown. Add color.

5

Completed Falcon.

Falcon

71

Duck

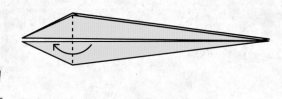

1

Start with Base Fold IV. Valley fold both front and back.

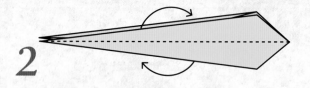

2

Valley fold to open flaps.

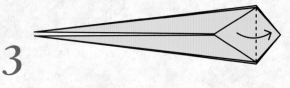

3

Valley fold both front and back.

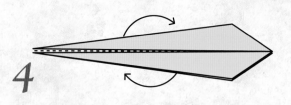

4

Valley fold both sides to return to position 2.

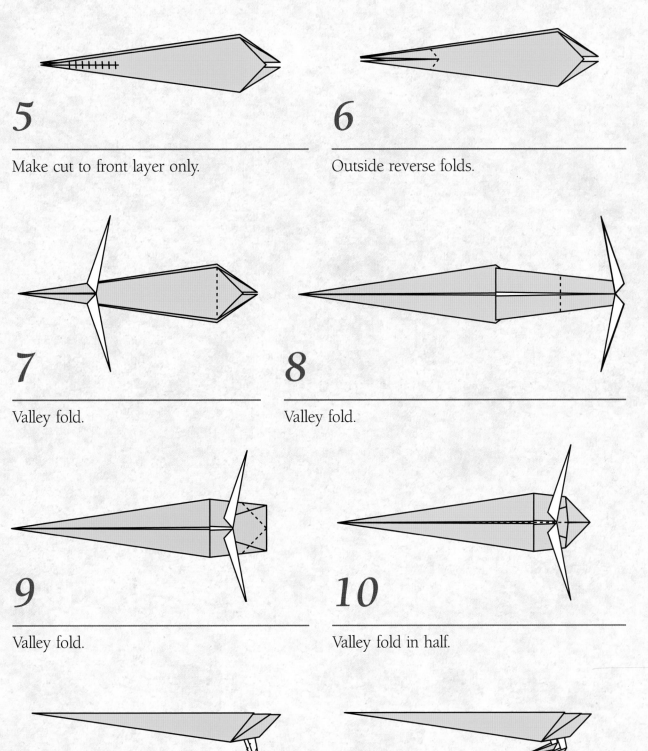

5

Make cut to front layer only.

6

Outside reverse folds.

7

Valley fold.

8

Valley fold.

9

Valley fold.

10

Valley fold in half.

11

Outside reverse folds.

12

See blow-ups for detail.

13

Inside reverse both sides.

14

Mountain fold both sides.

15

Valley fold each foot to side.

16

Valley fold both sides.

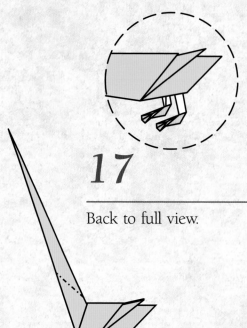

17

Back to full view.

18

Crimp fold.

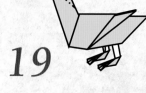

19

Inside reverse fold.

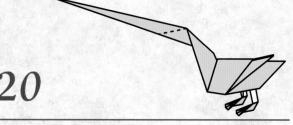

20

Outside reverse fold.

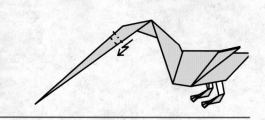

21

Pleat fold.

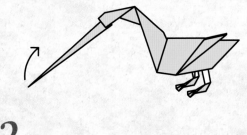

22

Pull in direction of arrow and crimp fold.

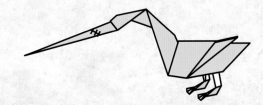

23

Cut as shown.

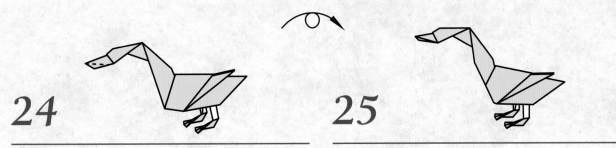

24

Valley fold both sides and rotate upright.

25

Add color and detail.

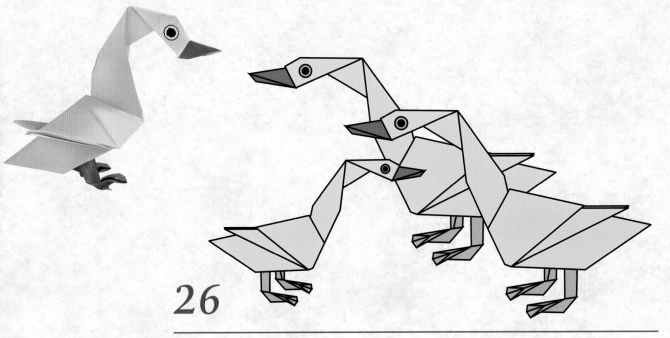

26

Completed Duck.

Toucan

Part 1

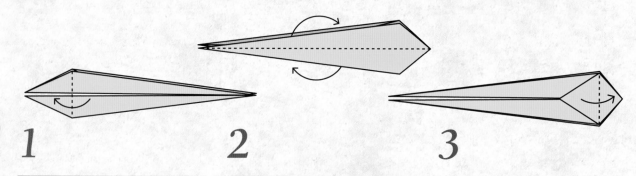

1

Start with Base Fold IV.
Valley fold front and back.

2

Valley fold to open flaps.

3

Valley fold both front and
back.

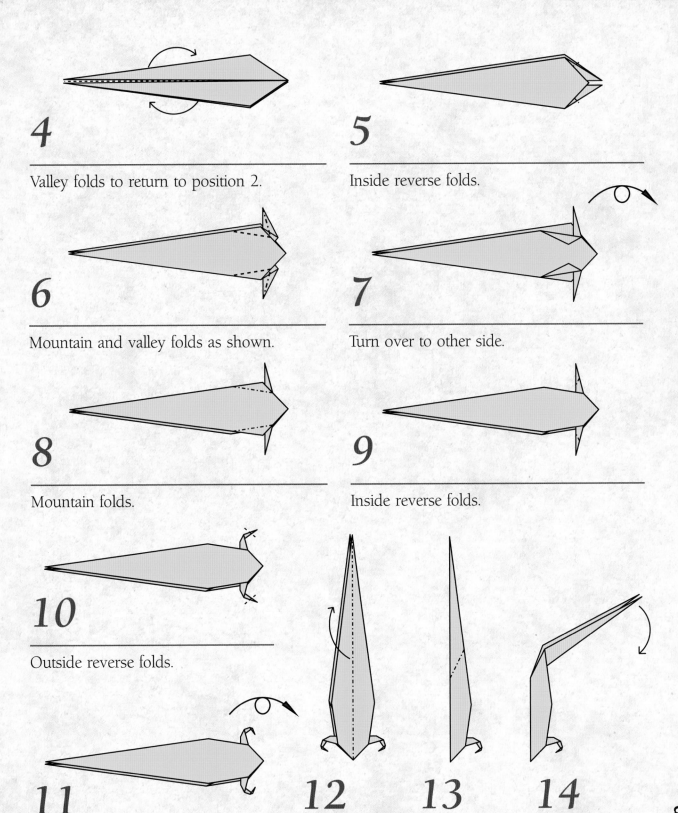

4

Valley folds to return to position 2.

5

Inside reverse folds.

6

Mountain and valley folds as shown.

7

Turn over to other side.

8

Mountain folds.

9

Inside reverse folds.

10

Outside reverse folds.

11

Rotate form.

12

Mountain fold in half.

13

Inside reverse fold.

14

Pull and squash fold.

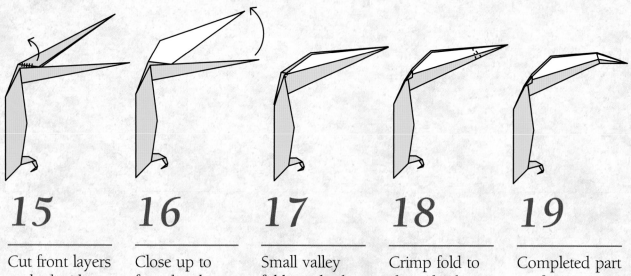

15

Cut front layers on both sides, then valley fold cut parts.

16

Close up to form head.

17

Small valley folds on both sides.

18

Crimp fold to shape beak.

19

Completed part 1 of toucan.

Part 2

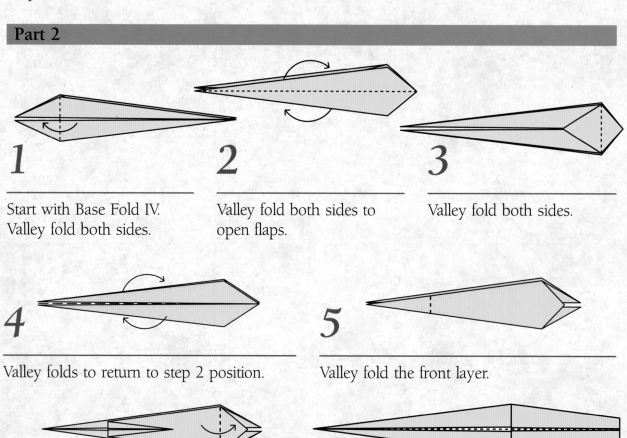

1

Start with Base Fold IV. Valley fold both sides.

2

Valley fold both sides to open flaps.

3

Valley fold both sides.

4

Valley folds to return to step 2 position.

5

Valley fold the front layer.

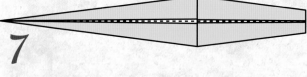

6

Valley fold in half.

7

Valley fold in half.

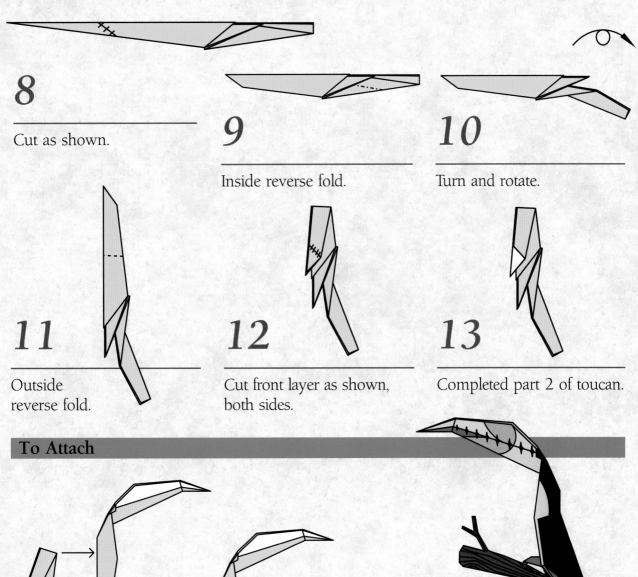

8

Cut as shown.

9

Inside reverse fold.

10

Turn and rotate.

11

Outside reverse fold.

12

Cut front layer as shown, both sides.

13

Completed part 2 of toucan.

To Attach

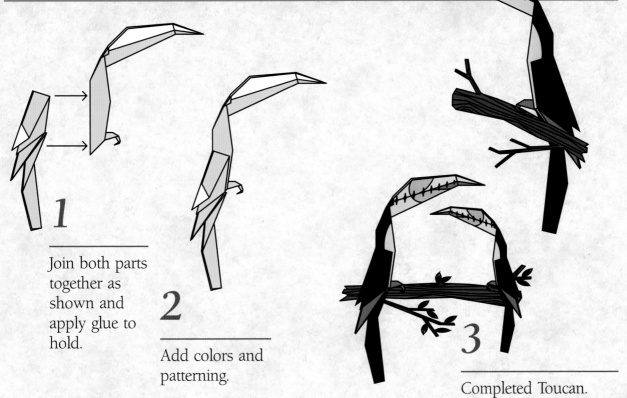

1

Join both parts together as shown and apply glue to hold.

2

Add colors and patterning.

3

Completed Toucan.

Cockatoo

Part 1

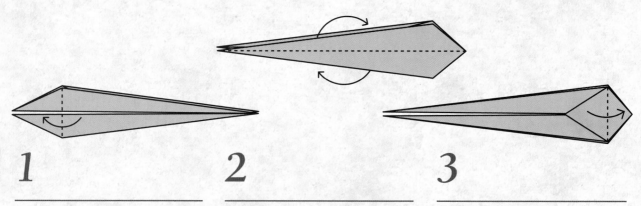

1

Start with Base Fold IV.
Valley folds front and back.

2

Valley fold both sides to
open flaps.

3

Valley folds both front and
back.

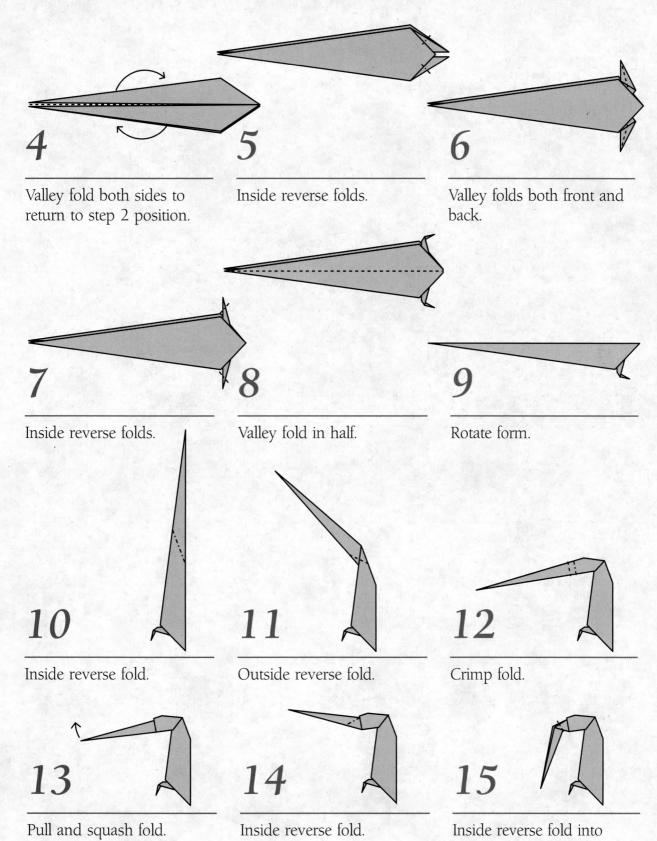

4

Valley fold both sides to return to step 2 position.

5

Inside reverse folds.

6

Valley folds both front and back.

7

Inside reverse folds.

8

Valley fold in half.

9

Rotate form.

10

Inside reverse fold.

11

Outside reverse fold.

12

Crimp fold.

13

Pull and squash fold.

14

Inside reverse fold.

15

Inside reverse fold into vertical position.

Cockatoo

16

Outside reverse fold.

17

Cut as shown, through both flaps.

18

Valley fold.

19

Turn over.

20

Valley fold.

21

Turn over.

22

Valley fold.

23

Turn over.

24

Valley fold.

25

Turn over.

26

Completed part 1 of cockatoo.

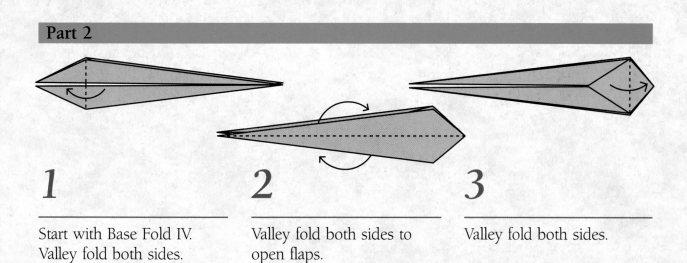

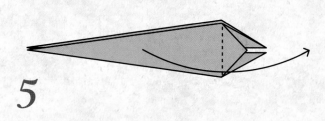

1

Start with Base Fold IV.
Valley fold both sides.

2

Valley fold both sides to
open flaps.

3

Valley fold both sides.

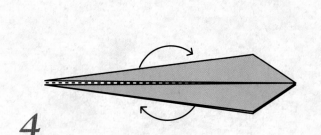

4

Valley fold sides back to step 2 position.

5

Valley fold as shown by arrow.

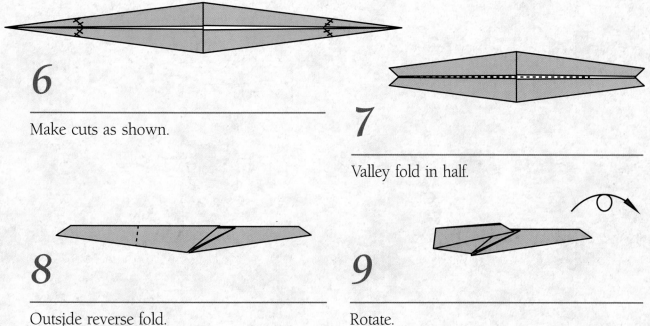

6

Make cuts as shown.

7

Valley fold in half.

8

Outside reverse fold.

9

Rotate.

Cockatoo

10

Valley fold wings and inside reverse fold.

11

Pull and squash fold to spread tail.

12

Completed part 2 of cockatoo.

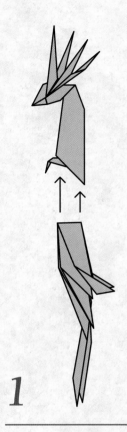

1

Join both parts together as shown and apply glue to hold.

2

Add colors and patterning.

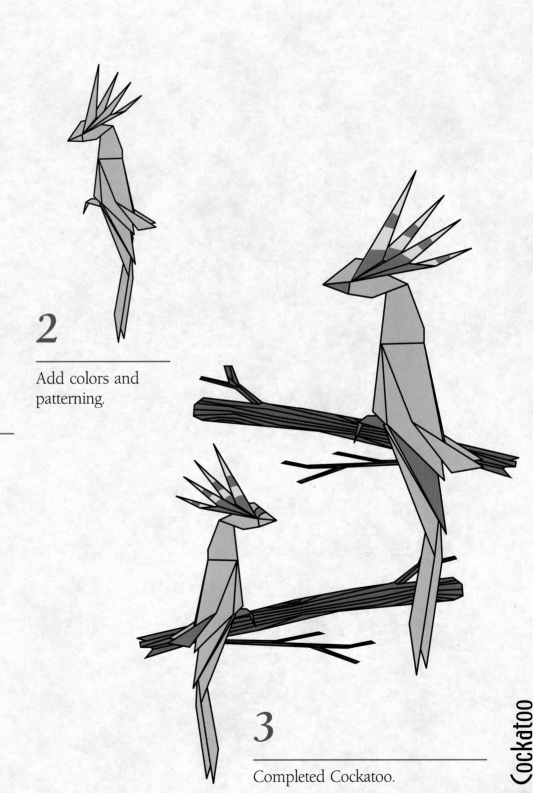

3

Completed Cockatoo.

Peacock

Part 1

1

Start with Base Fold IV. Valley fold both front and back.

2

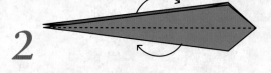

Valley fold both sides to open flaps.

3

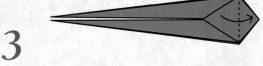

Valley fold both front and back.

4

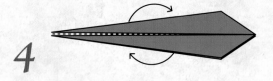

Valley fold both sides back to close flaps.

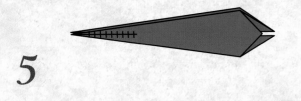

5

Cut front layer only as shown.

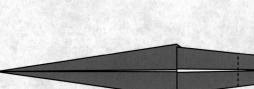

6

Outside reverse folds.

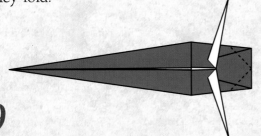

7

Valley fold.

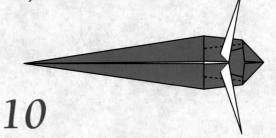

8

Valley folds.

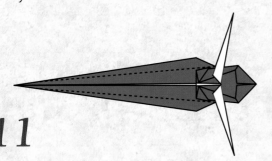

9

Valley folds.

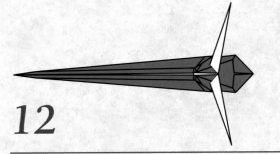

10

Valley folds.

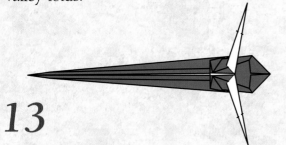

11

Valley folds.

12

Slip side flaps under front layers.

13

Outside reverse folds.

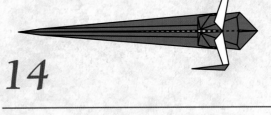

14

Valley fold in half.

Peacock

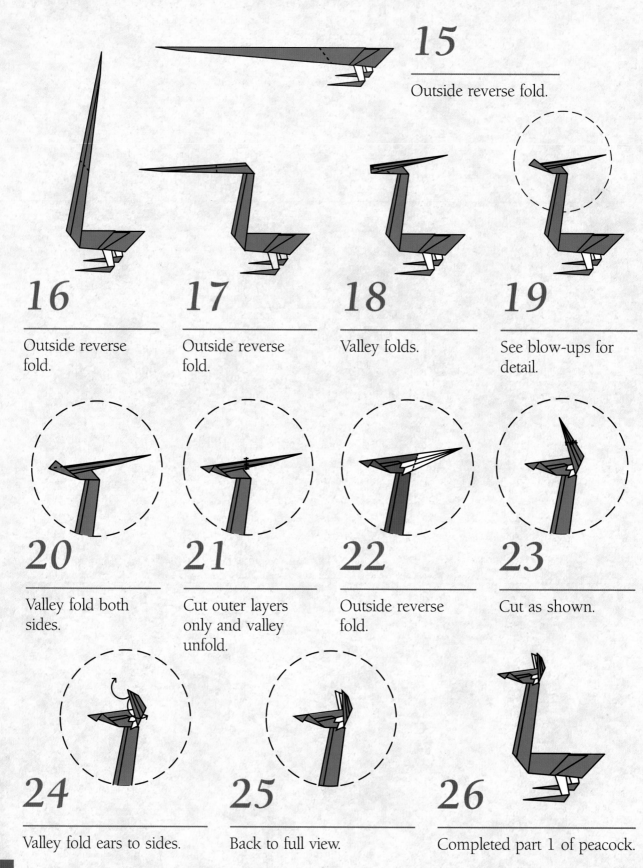

15

Outside reverse fold.

16

Outside reverse fold.

17

Outside reverse fold.

18

Valley folds.

19

See blow-ups for detail.

20

Valley fold both sides.

21

Cut outer layers only and valley unfold.

22

Outside reverse fold.

23

Cut as shown.

24

Valley fold ears to sides.

25

Back to full view.

26

Completed part 1 of peacock.

Peacock

1

Start with
a 4" by 4" square.

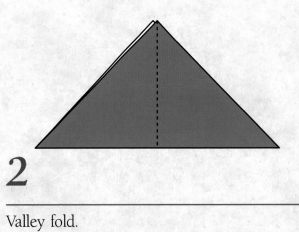

2

Valley fold.

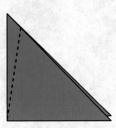

3

Valley fold to both
sides.

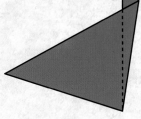

4

Repeat.

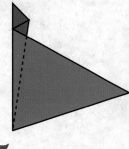

5

Valley to both sides
again.

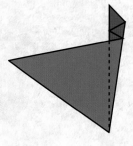

6

And again.

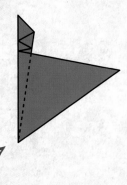

7

And again.

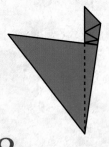

8

Keep valley folding
on both sides…

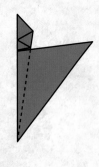

9

…until the paper
gets smaller…

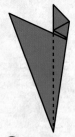

10

…and smaller…

Peacock

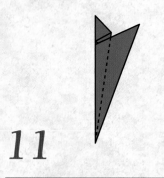 **11**

...until it won't fold anymore.

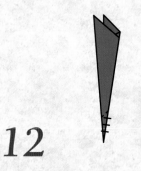 **12**

Cut partway up the fold as shown, and mountain fold both sides.

 **13**

Completed part 2 (tail) of peacock.

To Attach

 **1**

Open part 1 out to sides.

 **2**

Insert lower section of part 2 behind wings. Apply glue to hold.

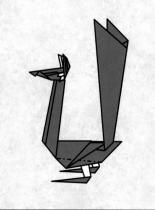 **3**

Mountain fold both sides.

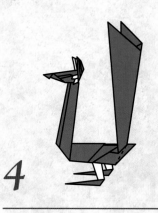 **4**

Outside reverse fold.

 **5**

Pull outer folds to open tail.

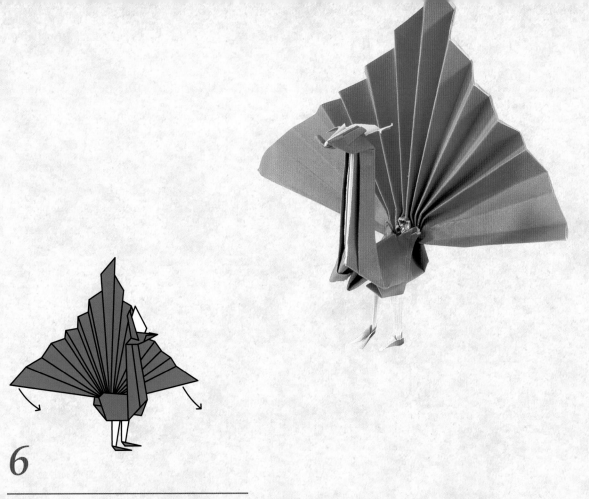

6

Pull sides of tail forward and squash fold into position.

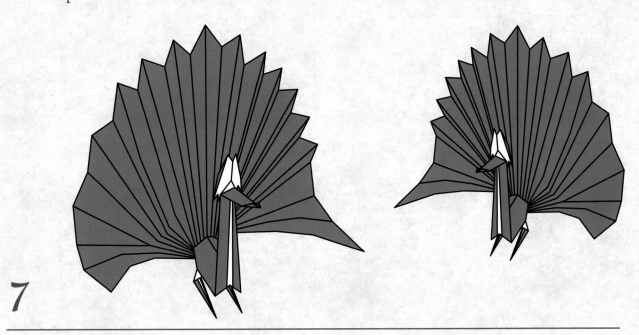

7

Completed Peacock.

Puffin

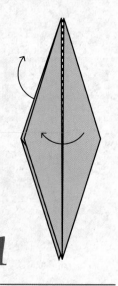

1

Start with Base
Fold III.

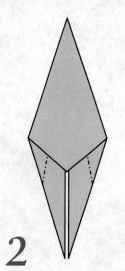

2

Inside reverse
folds.

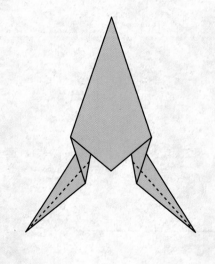

3

Valley folds.

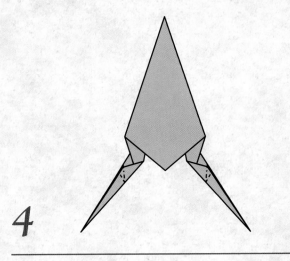

4

Crimp folds.

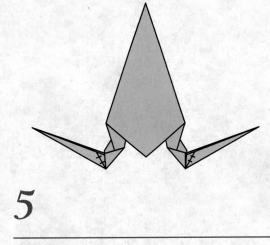

5

Cut, then valley open cut parts. Repeat behind.

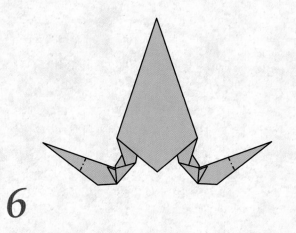

6

Inside reverse folds.

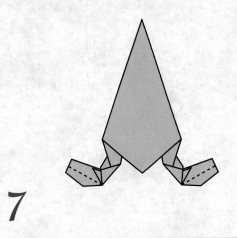

7

Valley folds to balance sides.

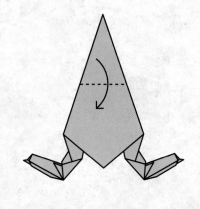

8

Valley fold.

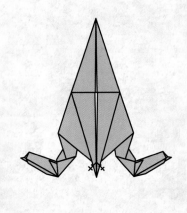

9

Cut as shown.

 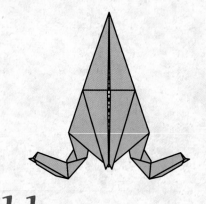 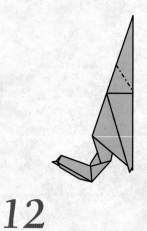

10

Make cuts to both sides.

11

Mountain fold in half.

12

Inside reverse fold.

 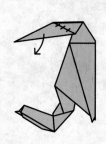 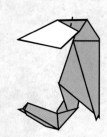

13

Outside reverse fold.

14

Cut each side, then valley open.

15

Valley fold both sides.

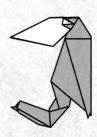 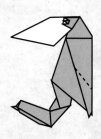 

16

Valley fold.

17

Outside reverse fold.

18

Rotate to upright.

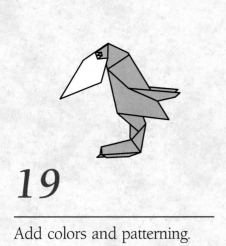

19

Add colors and patterning.

20

Completed Puffin.

Index